Toronto General Hospital

Toronto General Hospital By-Laws

Rules and Regulations - Adopted 1895

Toronto General Hospital

Toronto General Hospital By-Laws
Rules and Regulations - Adopted 1895

ISBN/EAN: 9783337158668

Printed in Europe, USA, Canada, Australia, Japan

Cover: Foto ©Suzi / pixelio.de

More available books at **www.hansebooks.com**

TORONTO

GENERAL HOSPITAL.

BY-LAWS, RULES

AND

REGULATIONS

ADOPTED, 1895

TORONTO:

ROWSELL AND HUTCHISON, PRINTERS

1895.

1895.

NURSES' HOME—TORONTO GENERAL HOSPITAL.

TORONTO GENERAL HOSPITAL.

ORIGINAL HOSPITAL, 1854-1878.

TORONTO GENERAL HOSPITAL.

Established 1819. – Incorporated by Act of Parliament, 18??

BY-LAWS AND RULES

OF THE

TORONTO GENERAL HOSPITAL.

Whereas by a statute passed in the sixteenth year of Her Majesty's reign, intitled " An Act to amend and consolidate the laws relating to the Toronto General Hospital," it is enacted, that the Trustees " shall and may from time to time, make such by-laws and rules for the internal management and regulation of the said Hospital, as shall to them seem meet and expedient; provided always, that such by-laws or rules shall be laid before the Lieutenant-Governor in Council, within thirty days after the same shall have been so made as aforesaid, and may be by him disallowed within one month thereafter."

And whereas it is considered desirable to provide more effectually for the internal management and regulation of the Hospital, and for other purposes herein contained, than the rules and regulations, made some years ago, provide for, ...

Therefore, the Trustees of the Toronto General Hospital, under and by virtue of said statute ; and under and by virtue of their general powers in law, make the following—

I.—BY-LAWS AND RULES.

1. All by-laws and rules relating to the persons and matters herein mentioned and provided for, and heretofore passed by the Trustees shall, after the making of these by-laws and rules, and after the expiration of one month from and after the time they are laid before the Lieutenant-Governor of Ontario in Council, and in case they are not by him disallowed within the said month, or after

His Honor's approval thereof, which ever event shall first happen, be repealed, in case no other time shall be declared for the same to take effect.

2. In case these by-laws and rules are not disallowed as aforesaid, the same shall take effect from and immediately after the repeal of the rules and regulations before mentioned.

3. In observance of an Act passed by the Ontario Legislature in 1868, the Board of Trustees shall consist of three Government Trustees, a representative chosen by subscribers to the Hospital funds,* and the Mayor of the city of Toronto (*ex off.*).

4. The Trustees shall elect a Chairman annually, when they appointed first take their seats as Trustees at a meeting duly called for the purpose, in case there is then a quorum, or as soon after as there is a quorum; and also whenever the Lieutenant-Governor appoints anew three Trustees according to the statute, and these persons first take their seats as Trustees, in case there is a quorum, or as soon after, as there is a quorum.

5. All meetings shall be presided over by the Chairman, or in his absence, by one of the other Trustees appointed for the occasion, by the other Trustees present.

6. The Trustees shall hold a general meeting monthly for the despatch of business, at which any business without special notice may be transacted.

7. All meetings shall be called by the Secretary by a printed or written notice, specifying the day, hour and place of the proposed meeting, which shall be delivered to or posted to each Trustee, directed to him by name at his usual place of business or residence, at least twenty-four hours (excluding Sundays) before the time of meeting.

8. The notice shall state whether it is a general or special meeting, and if a special meeting, what the object of the meeting is, in as short and general terms as will enable the Trustees to understand the nature of the business proposed to be considered or transacted; and

* Subscribers of $20 annually.

every such notice shall be signed by the Secretary, and be delivered or mailed by him as aforesaid.

9. They shall consider at a special meeting no other business than that of which notice has been given as aforesaid, unless all the Trustees are present and they all assent to other business being considered, in which case the additional business assented to, may be transacted, or the meeting may be ruled to be a general meeting if all the Trustees shall consent thereto, and general business may then be transacted thereat.

10. They shall, at any hour or day, visit the Hospital, and shall enter their names in a book at the Hospital, kept for that purpose.

11. They shall deposit or order the Secretary to deposit all moneys received on account of the Hospital, in one of the chartered banks of the Province, to the credit of the "Trustees of the Toronto General Hospital."

12. They shall not allow any money to be taken from such account, but by a cheque drawn on the bank, signed by the Chairman, or in his absence by the Chairman, *pro tem*, and countersigned by the Secretary, and no such check shall be signed, but by authority of the Trustees.

13. They shall invest in good and sufficient securities, all moneys which may at any time come into their hands, for the use and support of the Hospital, which may not be required by them for immediate expenditure or maintenance.

14. They shall from time to time, when required to do so, by the Lieutenant-Governor in Council, render an account in detail of all moneys received by them as Trustees, specifying the sources from which the same have arisen, or been received, and the manner in which the same have been invested and expended ; and all such other particulars as may be necessary to shew the state of the funds and endowment of the Hospital.

15. They shall prepare an annual statement of their affairs, and lay the same before the Legislature.

16. They shall prepare all other statements and reports,

which may be necessary, or which they may think expedient in the interest of the Hospital.

17. They shall appoint all such officers, assistants and others as they may think fit, or may find necessary for the purposes of the Hospital.

18. They shall fix the salaries and wages of all officers, and may alter the same from time to time as they may think fit.

19. They shall make all arrangements for the purchase of stores, medicine, food, clothing and other necessaries required for the use of the Hospital, or for the employees and patients thereof.

20. They shall provide for the due, faithful and economical management of the Hospital, and of all property belonging to it; and they shall lease such portions of the Hospital properties as they may think to be advantageous, and upon such terms and conditions as they may consider beneficial to the Hospital.

21. They shall see that all property belonging to the Trust, is properly preserved and repaired.

22. They shall endeavour to pay off the debenture debt, and to preserve the Hospital free from debt; and they shall see to the punctual payment of the interest on the debenture debt, and to the auditing and prompt payment of all accounts when vouched for and certified to be correct.

23. They may alter and limit from time to time, according to circumstances, the number and position of their officers, and prescribe and alter from time to time, when required, their respective duties.

24. They may provide for the delivery of clinical lectures in the Hospital by such persons, and at such times and on such terms and conditions as they may think proper, and for the admission thereto of students or such persons as they may direct.

25. They shall decide upon and limit from time to time, if necessary, the number of patients to be admitted into the Hospital, and the charge and terms upon which all paying patients shall be received and treated.

26. They may permit religious service or worship, scriptural or other proper readings to be had at such times, to such patients, and on such conditions as may be found convenient or expedient; but in no case shall any interference be allowed by any one, with the religious faith of any of the patients.

27. Any two of the Trustees may require the Secretary to call a special meeting at any time, stating to him the nature and object thereof.

28. The Chairman may call special meetings of the Trustees from time to time, in case he think it proper to do so.

29. The Chairman shall sign on behalf of the Trust all deeds, contracts, cheques, receipts and instruments which the Trustees may authorize to be executed, or which the corporation may be bound to execute.

30. The Trustees shall have power to make arrangements with any other Hospital Corporation for the acquisition thereof, or for the amalgamation thereof, with and under the name of the Toronto General Hospital Trust, provided that such terms and conditions shall not change or modify in any respect the present constitution of the governing body of the Toronto General Hospital Trust already created; and afrer the completion of such amalgamation, the amalgamated Corporation shall be managed and governed in every way as part and parcel of the "Toronto General Hospital Trust."

31. The Trustees shall have authority to take and hold real and personal estate which may be given, granted, bequeathed, or devised and accepted by the Trustees for the benefit of the Hospital, or any purpose connected therewith. Money received by them shall be invested under the direction of the Trustees; and all securities belonging to said corporation shall be placed in their custody; *provided* always, that both the principal and income thereof shall be appropriated according to the terms of the donation, devise or bequest, under the direction of said corporation.

14

32. They may do any other matter or thing, though not herein specially provided for, which may be within the scope of their authority, and within the spirit and *purview* of these by-laws, which they consider will be for the benefit of the Hospital or the welfare of the patients.

MEDICAL SUPERINTENDENT.

1. There shall be a Medical Superintendent, who shall be a regular registered Medical Practitioner, qualified under the Ontario Medical Act.

2. He shall be chief officer of the Institution, and shall be responsible to the Board of Trustees for the general management and government of the Institution.

3. He shall have the general supervision and charge of the Hospital and all officers, attendants, and employees of any kind, save and except the Secretary and his office assistants, who are directly under the supervision of the Trustees. He shall have the power of directing them in the discharge of their duties, and shall enforce discipline and good order in every department, and may suspend any employee who may be guilty of insubordination, disobedience or breach of rules, subject to the action of the Board of Trustees, such suspension to be reported immediately to the Chairman of the Board.

4. He shall direct and supervise all measures, of whatever nature, which may be necessary for the Medical or Surgical comfort, physical or moral improvement of the patients or inmates.

5. He shall inform himself as to the cleanliness, ventilation, heating and general sanitary condition of the wards and other portions of the buildings, and see that any defects are immediately remedied.

6. He shall regulate and determine the days and hours at which patients may be visited by friends or relations.

7. He shall see, as far as possible, that no insane person is admitted, and shall prevent as far as possible the admission of incurable and chronic cases, and he shall see that all

convalescent patients are discharged as soon as considered well enough to leave the Hospital.

8. He shall have power to dismiss any patient for improper conduct or breach of rules.

9. He shall see that the regulations and rules regarding the duties and attendance of the visiting Medical Staff are carried out, and that a record of the name of every Medical Officer of the Staff is duly entered in a book with the date and hour of each visit, and he shall report to the Board of Trustees any dereliction or neglect of duty on the part of any member of the Staff.

10. The Medical Superintendent (in the absence of the regular Visiting Physicians or Surgeons), shall act and give directions regarding the treatment of patients in the Hospital and shall notify the attending physician or surgeon in cases of emergency, without delay, or any other members of the Staff if considered necessary.

11. He shall not permit any major operation to be performed in the Hospital, except where delay might prove dangerous, without notifying the members of the Consulting and Surgical Staff, when the concurrence of the majority of those present must be obtained regarding the nature and extent of operation to be performed.

12. In emergency cases and accidents, the Medical Superintendent shall examine such patients brought to Hospital during the absence of or between regular visits of the Visiting Physicians or Surgeons, and shall give directions regarding treatment and prescribe for them, until seen by the respective members of the Staff under whose charge they are placed.

13. He shall attend the meetings of the Board of Trustees, whenever so required, for the purpose of consultation or to give information regarding the requirements of the Hospital, together with such suggestions and recommendations as he may deem desirable for the efficient medical and surgical treatment of the patients in the Hospital and the general management and good government of the Institution.

THE SECRETARY.

1. The Secretary shall give such security as may be deemed requisite by the Trustees for the due accounting for and payment of all moneys which he may from time to time receive or pay out by order of the Board.

2. The Secretary shall attend all meetings of the Trustees and Committees of the Board, take and keep minutes of the proceedings of each meeting, and transcribe the same into minute book.

3. Through him all communications shall be made to the Trustees, and by him from the said Trustees to the public or any department of the Hospital, unless otherwise ordered.

4. One day previous to each and every meeting of the Trustees, it shall be his duty to send notice of the time and place of meeting to each Trustee, and on extraordinary occasions to state the purpose of the meeting, conformable to the By-law number seven, chapter two, before mentioned.

5. The Secretary shall have the custody of the seal of corporation

6. He shall keep the necessary books for entering all transactions of the Trustees.

7. He shall keep a regular and strict account of the Income and Expenditure of the Institution, balance the same monthly, and lay the same upon the table at the meeting of the Trustees next ensuing

8. He shall lay all accounts, statements and reports of every matter concerning the Hospital, or the estate, property or funds of the Trust, or the employees or patients, and every other matter or thing necessary for the Trustees to be informed of, before the Trustees at each of their meetings.

9. He shall collect promptly all rents, interest, moneys due by pay-patients, or other income due to the Trust; and shall also promptly maintain all necessary insurances, and pay all claims against the Trust with the moneys which

may be furnished to him by the Trustees for the purpose, and shall take a receipt for all moneys which he pays out.

10. He shall keep a stock book in which shall be entered in detail a list of all the furniture, bedding, linen, utensils of all descriptions, and all other the personal chattels of the Hospital, and he shall furnish such persons in the Hospital, as the Trustees shall direct, with a copy thereof; and shall report on the same to the Trustees once every year.

11. He shall keep in safe places, provided for the purpose, all deeds, leases, contracts, accounts, receipts, reports, books, plans, and other documents of, or relating to the Hospital.

12. He shall take charge of all valuables, money, and effects of patients dying in the Hospital which may not be claimed by the family, relatives, or connections of the deceased, or by any other person authorized to receive the same.

13. He shall countersign all cheques drawn on the bank for money; and he shall also sign all deeds, leases and contracts of or relating to the Hospital or the property thereof.

14. He shall pay the salary and wages of the employees, and shall receive his own salary at the same time as the other employees are paid.

15. He shall keep an employees' receipt book, in which all moneys paid to the employees shall be entered, and in which they shall be required to receipt the same as they are respectively paid.

LADY SUPERINTENDENT AND SUPERINTENDENT OF TRAINING SCHOOL FOR NURSES.

1. There shall be a Lady Superintendent and Superintendent of Training School, who must hold a certificate from a recognized "Training School for Nurses." She shall have general charge and supervision of all that is directly connected with the domestic economy of the Hospital, and shall have charge of all nurses, including their practical instruction and teaching in the Training School. She shall supervise all nursing work, and shall observe carefully the manner in which nurses and orderlies care for the sick. She is charged with the responsibility of the Nurses' Home, and the instruction of nurses in the Training School, and shall, with the approval of the Medical Superintendent, prescribe courses of study, lectures and examinations, during their terms of service, and shall make all necessary rules for the government of nurses and education of nurses in the Training School. She shall, with the approval of the Medical Superintendent, select suitable applicants as probationers, and shall suspend or dismiss any probationer or nurse for cause, with the approval of the Medical Superintendent only. She shall, with the approval of the Chairman of Board and Medical Superintendent, arrange for the appointment of examiners at stated periods, whose duty it shall be to examine each and every candidate, and report on their qualifications before they can or shall receive the certificate of the Training School as skilled nurses. She shall, with the concurrence of Medical Superintendent, arrange and assign all duties connected with the different employees under her care. She shall see that all parts of the Hospital, beds and bedding are sufficiently supplied and kept clean and in good order. She shall report any repairs required to the Medical Superintendent. She shall see that all employees and nurses, under her charge are dressed in a neat and clean manner, and that they are at all times attentive to their various duties.

2. That all stores under her care are given out and distributed as required, and that there is no improper or unnecessary waste.

3. She shall arrange the hours of meals and the hours for duty of all nurses and employees in her department, also the hours of retiring at night and rising in the morning.

4. She shall report any illness of nurses or servants to the Medical Superintendent, who will, if necessary, see that they are prescribed for.

5. She shall see that a proper supply of medical and surgical dressings and appliances are kept by Head Nurse in the supply closet of each Surgical Ward, the closet to be kept always locked by Head Nurse.

6. She shall report to the Medical Superintendent any articles which, in her opinion, may be required for the Hospital.

7. She shall make frequent visits to all parts of the Hospital wards, bed-rooms, kitchens, laundry, nurses' rooms and dining-rooms, by day and occasionally at night.

8. She shall report to the Medical Superintendent any misconduct on part of patients or employees, or any irregularity coming under her notice. She shall keep all wine, beer, spirits and liquors under lock and key, under her own personal charge, and shall deliver out the same for use as required by order in the diet book, or upon special written order of any of the Medical staff in cases of emergency only.

9. She shall give timely notice to the Medical Superintendent or Steward, when any stores or liquors under her charge, are nearly exhausted or require to be replenished.

10. She shall keep an account of the nurses', servants', and other employees' time and wages in her department, and notify the Secretary of such every month. She shall, with concurrence of the Medical Superintendent, suspend or dismiss any nurse or employee guilty of insubordination or breach of rules.

11. She shall have the charge and supervision of the

3

nurses both when on and off duty, including their instruction in the Training School; their duties, as well, when nursing in private families as in the Hospital; and the maintenance of proper discipline and becoming conduct at all times.

12. She shall not be absent from the Hospital over night or for any lengthened period without the knowledge of the Medical Superintendent, or in his absence the Chairman of the Board.

ASSISTANT TO LADY SUPERINTENDENT.

1. She shall perform all necessary duties assigned to her by the Lady Superintendent, either in connection with the Hospital or in the Training School for Nurses, and shall report any irregularity which may come under her notice to the Lady Superintendent, or in her absence to the Medical Superintendent.

2. She shall not absent herself from the Hospital without the permission of the Lady Superintendent, or in her absence the Medical Superintendent.

RESIDENT MEDICAL ASSISTANTS.

Resident assistants are appointed annually, and hold their positions for one year. They are selected from the graduates every spring and are on duty in the Surgical wards, Medical wards, Burnside, Eye and Ear department, Gynæcological and Extern department, wards for Infectious Diseases, the Dispensary and Pathological department, for such periods as the Medical Superintendent may arrange.

GENERAL RULES FOR RESIDENT MEDICAL ASSISTANTS.

1. The Assistants are to perform all duties assigned to them by the Medical Superintendent.

2. It is their duty to visit all the patients allotted to them at least twice a day, and oftener if necessary ; to inform themselves fully of the condition of each patient admitted to the wards in their charge as soon as possible after admission, so as to be able to answer inquiries; to assist Physicians or Surgeons in charge of the cases, and see that directions regarding diet and treatment are fully carried out; to keep notes of all cases ; and to communicate promptly with the Medical Superintendent respecting anything proper to be brought under his notice, particularly matters affecting the comfort of the patients, insubordination, or neglect of duty by, any of the attendants.

3. In the absence of the Medical Superintendent, one of the Assistants (whose turn it is to be on special duty) shall remain in or near the general office to admit patients, attend cases of emergency, and perform such other services as may be requisite.

4. The Assistants are to take part, when so required, in admitting out-door patients in any department.

5. No Assistant is to absent himself from the Hospital before *4.30 o'clock p.m.*, without permission from the Medical Superintendent, and when leaving the premises must arrange with his colleagues for the performance in his absence of all ordinary and regular duties.

6. One half of the number of Assistants must always remain on duty. This rule is imperative.

7. The Assistants are relied upon to co-operate in promoting harmony, discipline, and the general efficiency and good name of the Hospital and the Training School, by every means in their power, and particularly by their own conduct, demeanor, and example, whether on or off active duty. They are especially cautioned against attentions to, or familiarity with, any of the nurses, not only as a viola-

tion of the rules of the Training School, but also as unbecoming in their respective positions in the Hospital, as interfering with proper discipline, and as tending to injure the nurse, by diverting attention from her work in the wards and in the School, and to prejudice her in her standing with the Hospital authorities. This caution applies outside, as well as in the Hospital premises, and neglect of it, will render the offender liable to instant dismissal.

8. Each Assistant must furnish himself with a surgical pocket case and stethoscope.

DISPENSING ASSISTANT.

1. The Assistant in charge of the Dispensary is to compound and make up all medicines according to the written prescriptions of the Physicians, for both in-door and out-door patients: to deliver medicines for distribution at hours designated by the Medical Superintendent, and at other times when required in special cases: to put up all medicines carefully, and attach a label to every bottle, box, or powder, etc., with name of patient, number of ward, and full directions regarding dose and *administration.* No medicine shall be allowed to leave the Dispensary without a label, and great care must be exercised in putting on the proper labels, viz., blue labels for medicines to be used externally, lotions, liniments, etc., and yellow labels for medicines to be taken by the *mouth* only. He is also to keep the Dispensary and appliances in good order and neat, and carefully observe economy in every thing relating to the department: to permit no one to enter the Dispensary unnecessarily: to put in a written requisition daily to the Medical Superintendent of all goods and drugs required for the Dispensary: and to examine and check invoices on arrival of all stores.

2. It shall be the duty of the Assistant in charge of the Dispensary to prescribe for nurses and servants when so requested by the Medical or Lady Superintendent or Housekeeper.

3. Medicines are not to be delivered to the patients themselves, either when remaining in, or when about to leave the Hospital.

N.B.—The utmost prudence and care must be exercised in making up and giving directions regarding all medicines.

The following agreement must be signed immediately after appointment as Assistant—is made by the Trustees:

I, the undersigned..................................... having read the above rules and regulations, do hereby accept the position of Resident Assistant, and agree to observe all the rules of the Hospital, and I promise faithfully to remain on duty until June 15th, 1895.

. . . .

Witness:

. . . .

The following form of application must be signed and filled in by applicant:—

TORONTO,   189

To Chairman and Trustees of
     Toronto General Hospital:

GENTLEMEN,—

I hereby apply for a position on the Resident Staff of Medical Assistants at Toronto General Hospital for the year 189 -9 .

I am at the present time an undergraduate of
                and expect to graduate therefrom in Spring of 189 . It is my intention also, to present myself at the Ontario Medical Council Examination to be held in April, 189 . If appointed, I agree to keep and observe all the rules and regulations of the Hospital, and I promise faithfully to remain on duty until June 15th, 189 .

I have the honor to be,
Your obedient servant,

Name in full ....

Age ....

Nativity ....

Residence ....

School ....

P.S.—Formal applications should be handed in as soon as possible after the Christmas vacation, as applications will not be received after the results of the final examinations are declared. Certificates as to character or ability, and all letters of recommendation as to professional standing, etc., can be sent in at any time prior to the appointments being finally made.

HOUSEKEEPER.

1. The Housekeeper shall have the general oversight and charge of cleanliness of the whole establishment, with the Nurses' Home and Laundry.

2. She shall also be responsible for the cleanliness of the private rooms, officers' and servants' rooms, offices, theatre, halls, lobbies and corridors, and shall inspect and take proper care of the linen, beds, bedding, furniture, etc., in the different rooms under her care.

3. She shall have charge of all female servants, porters (male), laundry men, upholsterer; attend to their department, see that they do their work and are on duty at 7 a.m.

4. See that all servants are in rooms at 10 p.m. and lights out at 10.30 p.m.

5. Superintend kitchen, cooking, serving of food, and prevent waste.

6. Provide medical aid when servants are ill.

7. Discharge and hire servants when necessary, giving and receiving two weeks' notice.

8. With approval of Lady Superintendent, make rules necessary for the proper conduct and efficient service of all employees in her department.

9. Keep a book with names of servants, time engaged, amount paid, time off, holidays, etc., and make a report monthly to Lady Superintendent.

10. Give supplies out of delf room, keeping account of same in a book.

11. Attend to ventilation of basement and servants' rooms.

12. Supervise night nurses' supper.

13. Have charge of general sewing, manufacture of bedding, and clothing and other supplies, and attend to repairs and marking of clothes before they leave the linen room.

14. Conduct morning prayers with servants.

15. Attend to exchanges in Nurses' Home, kitchen, etc., on last Friday in each month.

16. She shall also see that all articles requiring fumigation, such as clothing, bedding, etc., are properly sterilized and returned to the wards from which they were sent.

Head Cook.

1. Duties include the safe-keeping and economical use of all supplies issued, the cooking and distribution among the several tables or wards according to regular dietary, with attention to extras ordered for patients, and with care to prevent food or extras being misappropriated.

2. She is to see that the kitchen and utensils are kept clean and in good order, and that unused supplies are returned to the kitchen immediately after meals, and to check all wastefulness, particularly seeing that no food or supplies of any kind are taken from the kitchen or hospital by any assistant servant or patient.

3. She will belong to the Housekeeper's department and must report promptly to the Housekeeper, or to the Medical Superintendent, or Lady Superintendent, any matter requiring special attention, and particularly any misconduct,

insubordination, or neglect of duty on part of her subordinates.

HEAD LAUNDRESS.

1. The Head Laundress shall have charge of the Laundry, and shall receive and be responsible for all the soiled clothes being properly washed, dried, aired, and returned to linen room or wards.

2. She shall be responsible for the cleanliness and neatness of the department (except the engine, boiler, machinery, and coal rooms), and the good conduct of those detailed to assist her.

3. She shall permit no person (not employed there) to visit the Laundry, except by permission of the Lady Superintendent, and shall report immediately to the Lady Superintendent, any of her assistants, who are insubordinate or neglectful in their duty.

4. She shall see that the soap, starch, and all other stores entrusted to her care are economically used, and that no stores or provisions of any kind are taken out of the Laundry.

THE LAUNDRY-MAIDS.

1. The Laundry-maids shall perform all the washing, ironing, etc., for the establishment, and be responsible for every article delivered to them, until returned in a condition suitable for immediate use.

2. They shall be under the superintendence of the Head Laundress, and shall not leave the Laundry without her permission during hours of duty.

THE FEMALE SERVANTS.

1. They shall be under the immediate charge of the Housekeeper and subject to her control.

2. They shall obey the directions of the Housekeeper, and perform all work assigned to them, in the manner and at the time specified. They shall not absent themselves from the Hospital without the permission of the Housekeeper.

3. All servants must be promptly on duty at 7 a.m. They must not remain out without permission after 10 p.m., at which hour they are expected to be in their rooms and all lights out.

4. Any case of illness must be at once reported to the Lady Superintendent, and nothing can be obtained from the Dispensary without an order.

5. All household supplies must be obtained from the Linen Room between the hours of 9 and 10 a.m.

6. Servants may see their friends in the Sitting Room assigned them, but in no other part of the building.

7. Loud talking, laughing, and all unnecessary noise in wards and corridors strictly forbidden.

8. Servants are not to hold any communication with any patients, while in the Hospital. They must not take them food nor drink, nor visit the wards without permission from Lady Superintendent.

9. A vacation of one week will be allowed in each year of service: for all other time off duty, a deduction will be made from the monthly pay.

10. Any servant being disobedient or violating any rules is liable to instant dismissal, without the usual two weeks' notice.

The Kitchen-Maids.

1. The Kitchen-maids shall assist the Cook in the performance of their duties, as may be directed by the Housekeeper, and generally aid in the discharge of the various duties of the kitchen.

THE STEWARD.

1. The Steward shall have the general oversight of the Hospital premises, including buildings, grounds, property, and stores of all kinds, except medical and surgical supplies and appliances, wines or liquors.

2. He shall purchase stores and supplies in the manner directed by the Board of Trustees or Medical Superin-

tendent; and it shall be his duty to see to their proper care, use, and distribution.

3. He shall examine and check all invoices, and weigh or measure all stores received.

4. He shall keep a stock book in which he shall enter all stores received, and at the end of each month the stores on hand.

5. He shall see, as far as possible, that all the buildings and premises are kept in proper order and repair, and for this purpose shall make regular visits to all parts of the premises, and shall report any repairs required to the Medical Superintendent.

6. He shall particularly see to the cleanliness and good order of all the store rooms, and the basement.

7. He shall have the direction of all the male attendants in his department, mechanics, and other persons employed in or about the Hospital.

8. The patients' and servants' dining-room shall be under his direct supervision. He is to attend to the carving and distribution of food sent from the dining-rooms to the wards and to the proper serving and carving of the meals taken in the dining-rooms ; or these duties may, under his direction, be discharged by his assistant if qualified.

9. He is not to absent himself from the premises, except on the regular business of his department, without leave of the Medical Superintendent.

10. He is in the discharge of all his duties to be under the immediate direction of the Medical Superintendent.

11. He is promptly to report to the Medical Superintendent any misconduct, neglect of duty, or irregularity which may come under his notice on the part of any servant, patient, or other inmate of the Institution.

STEWARD'S MEN OR STORE-KEEPERS.

The Store-keepers shall assist the Steward in the receiving, care, and issuing of stores and supplies, and shall perform such other clerical duties as the Medical Superintendent or Steward shall require.

ENGINEER.

1. The Engineer shall have the care of all boilers, furnaces, stoves, grates, steam and water pipes, and other apparatus belonging to the heating of any of the buildings ; all steam engines and machinery used in the laundry or elsewhere ; fire plugs, fire hose, hydrants, and appurtenances connected with the water and gas services in the buildings or anywhere upon the grounds or premises ; all gas metres, pipes, and connections ; all baths, closets, water tanks, hot water fixtures and appliances; and is to see that they are kept in good order, doing himself all ordinary repairs and reporting to the Medical Superintendent all extraordinary repairs required in his department; and for this purpose he is to regularly inspect and examine the premises.

2. He is to maintain a temperature of at least 65° throughout the wards both day and night during cold or changeable weather.

3. He is to receive and weigh all coal and certify to the correctness of all invoices of coal delivered ; and is to see that it is used economically.

4. He shall be responsible for the cleanliness and order of all parts and rooms under his care.

5. No patient or other person (not having business there) shall be allowed to be in the boiler-rooms or workshops, or to loiter about in any part of the basement. The Engineer is to enforce this rule, and is to report any breach of it or any other irregularity to the Medical Superintendent.

6. All articles required for the department are to be obtained by requisition from Medical Superintendent.

7. He is held personally responsible for the good order

of all hose and fire appliances, and shall instruct all officers, nurses and employees regarding the use of such for fire purposes.

THE JANITOR.

1. The Janitor shall be on his station in the main hall from 7 o'clock in the morning during summer, and from 8 o'clock in winter. He shall keep the reception hall neat; he shall attend to all visitors, receive and convey all letters, papers, telegrams or messages to the officers and patients.

2. He shall answer all telephone messages.

3. He shall ring the bell at the regular bed hours, when visitors shall leave the wards and Hospital.

MECHANICS AND MALE EMPLOYEES.

The gardeners, carpenters, painters, upholsterers, firemen, laundrymen, deck hands, and all other male employees, are under the regular rules and discipline of the Hospital, according to the department to which they are attached, and shall perform all duties assigned them at any time by the Medical Superintendent or Steward.

NIGHT SUPERINTENDENT OF NURSES.

1. The Night Superintendent of Nurses shall, under the direction of the Superintendent of Nurses, have general charge of all nursing in the Hospital between the hours of 9 p.m. and 7 a.m. She shall see that all nurses and Ward Tenders on night duty are prompt, faithful and watchful in the discharge of their duties; shall attend to the warmth and ventilation of the wards, and to the proper use of the gas; shall be watchful against accidents from fire; and shall give special attention to patients dangerously ill, and to all exigencies which may arise during the night.

7. It shall be the duty of the Ward Tenders to report promptly to the Head Nurse anything requiring attention, and any misbehaviour or insubordination of patients or persons employed. The omission to do this will be considered a serious offence.

8. Ward Tenders shall be on hand promptly to move patient to the Operating Theatre at the appointed hours. All directions of the Medical Officers and Head Nurses must be carefully noted and obeyed, and all patients must be treated kindly by Ward Tenders.

9. Ward Orderlies must give male patients a bath upon admission, unless the contrary is distinctly ordered by the House Physician or Surgeon, and all male patients must have a full bath each week, unless otherwise ordered ; but never sooner than two hours after a meal.

10. The affairs and condition of all patients, are to be considered as strictly private.

11. Upon admission to the wards, patients should invariably be informed by the Ward Tender in charge, that valuables can be kept in the wards only at the risk of the owners. All valuables must be handed to Head Nurse and kept in the safe in the office, as the Trustees refuse to assume any responsibility for losses which may occur.

12. In no case shall any property of patients (including clothing) be delivered to anyone other than the owner without an order from the office.

13. No attempts to regulate excessive heat or cold should be made in the wards. The thermometer must be watched, and when the temperature of the ward falls below 62 degrees, or rise above 68 degrees, in cold weather, it must be reported at once to the Engineer.

14. Ward Tenders or Orderlies are not to visit female wards or talk with nurses or servants when on duty, except in performance thereof.

15. At the discretion of the Lady Superintendent, Ward Tenders will be allowed leave of absence one afternoon in each week. They will also be excused from duty a part of each Sunday. They will have permission to be absent one

evening in each week, but must not be out after 10 o'clock
without special permission. They shall have a vacation of
one week in each year, the time of which shall be determined according to the exigencies of the Hospital service,
with due regard to their wishes and convenience.

16. Ward Tenders or Orderlies must not apply for leave
at times which will interfere with the regular hours of
others, nor will leave be granted on the regularly appointed
visiting or operating days.

17. In case of illness, Ward Tenders are expected to
report at once to the Lady Superintendent, who will see that
Medical aid is procured when such is required. No Ward
Tender shall be permitted to occupy a bed in any of the
wards without the consent of the Medical Superintendent.

MEDICAL STAFF.

1. The Trustees of the Toronto General Hospital are
authorized to appoint from the members of the medical
profession practising in Toronto a Medical Staff, to hold
their positions at the pleasure of the Trustees, but to ter-
minate on the 30th day of June in each year, any member
of the Staff to be eligible for re-appointment; and the
Trustees may pass by-laws, regulating the duties of the
Staff and matters of routine relating to medical attendance.

The Staff shall consist of two divisions, to be called the
Consulting Staff and the Active Staff.

2. They shall, with the Resident Staff, constitute the
Medical and Surgical Staff of the Hospital.

Consulting Physicians and Surgeons.

Visiting Physicians.

Visiting Surgeons.

Visiting Ophthalmic and Aural Surgeons, who shall also
be Aural and Ophthalmic Surgeons to out-patients.

Physicians to out-patients.

Surgeons to out-patients.

Physicians for Diseases of Women, including Gynæ-
cology and Obstetrics.

Physicians for Diseases of the Throat and Nose.
Pathologists—Electricians.
Registrars.
Dentists.

3. The Trustees may also annually appoint Medical and Surgical Assistants from members of extern staff to assist on intern staff, when required.

4. The term of office of all members of the Visiting Medical and Surgical Staff and Assistants shall begin on the first day of July and continue one year.

5. In case a vacancy shall occur on the Medical, Surgical or Assistants Staff, the Trustees may fill the same for the residue of the unexpired term.

6. The Trustees may also, from time to time, appoint such other officers or specialists as may be necessary.

7. They may, at their pleasure, remove or discharge any member of the Staff appointed by them.

8. They may fill any vacancy which occurs, for the residue of the unexpired term, in the manner in which the original appointment was made.

9. They shall fix the duties of all Medical officers so appointed or employed; but no compensation shall be received by, or given to members of the Visiting Medical and Surgical Staff or Assistants for their services to the Hospital.

10. They shall make, from time to time, such rules for the general efficiency of the Medical and Surgical service of the Hospital as may seem expedient to them.

CONSULTING PHYSICIANS AND SURGEONS.

The Trustees may appoint to the Consulting Staff any person who has served for at least six years on the Active Staff.

The Consulting Physicians and Surgeons shall be invited to attend all capital operations in the Hospital, and to examine and give advice on all such critical or special cases as the attending Physicians and Surgeons or Specialists may desire.

VISITING PHYSICIANS AND SURGEONS.

1. The Attending Physicians and Surgeons shall make such arrangements as to the division of patients so that one Physician and Surgeon shall visit every medical and surgical patient who may be afflicted with an acute disease, at least once every day, and every patient in the Hospital, under his care, without exception, twice in every week. When members of the active Staff are unable to visit the Hospital regularly on account of illness, absence from the city, or other reasons, new patients shall not be admitted under their care for the time being, or until they are able personally to resume duty.

2. All patients in the Hospital will be under the care of the regular Medical Staff, except as may be provided for or otherwise allowed by the Trustees.

3. There shall be a separation of the service into Medical, Surgical, Gynæcological, Opthalmological, Laryngological and Obstetrical divisions ; and one or two of the members in charge of each division, as may be expedient, shall be on duty constantly, alternating, according to the arrangements made and agreed upon.

4. They shall direct the House Physicians and Surgeons to report to the Medical Superintendent such patients as are in proper condition to leave the Hospital.

5. It shall be their duty during their respective times of attendance to prescribe and direct the treatment of patients under their care ; but in case of emergency, admitting of no delay, the attending Physician or Surgeon being absent, the Medical Superintendent or House Physicians or Surgeons shall prescribe and report to the attending Physician or Surgeon at their first visit.

6. At each visit the Medical Officer shall write such prescriptions, and give such directions as he may deem necessary to the Medical Superintendent, Assistants and others with respect to his patients.

7. Each Medical Officer shall keep, or cause his Clinical Clerk or Dresser to keep, a case book, in which shall be entered an account of each patient admitted under him

into the Hospital, the name, age, and occupation of such patient ; the history and probable cause of the disease, the daily changes and such other notes as may tend to throw light on the nature of the case, with prescriptions of treatment.

8. The visiting hour shall be at 2.30 o'clock p.m., daily, throughout the year, except Sunday.

9. They shall not admit for treatment any insane person or lunatic, unless the same arise from *delirium tremens*, or other ordinarily curable disease.

10. No capital operation shall be performed, except in cases where delay might be dangerous, without giving notice thereof to all the Surgeons belonging to the Hospital, nor without the concurrence of the majority of those present. The nature and position of the operation to be performed, shall also be determined in the same manner.

11. All licensed Practitioners may walk the wards in company with the visiting Medical Officer at the usual hour, and may attend all operations; but they shall not dictate or interfere in the practice.

12. Each attending Physician or Surgeon shall confine his attention, when visiting the Hospital, to patients belonging to his own department, unless when requested by a colleague to examine or prescribe for a patient belonging to another department.

13. If any Physician or Surgeon shall be prevented from attending in his turn, he shall notify the Medical Superintendent of his inability, in order that arrangements may be made to look after his patients during his absence.

14. In order to render the Hospital (so far as may consist with the welfare of the patients), conducive to the advancement of medical science, the Physicians and Surgeons may provide adequate and regular instruction by observations accompanying operations and prescriptions by clinical lectures or otherwise, to students properly admitted to see the practice of the Hospital. It shall be the duty of the Physician and Surgeon to guard against any examination of patients by pupils, except under his own directions,

and against all acts calculated to alarm or injure patients. In cases where any observations in their presence might have an injurious tendency they shall be postponed to the halls or theatre of the Hospital. Clinical bedside classes must not exceed twenty students in each class.

15. The visiting Medical Staff shall report to the Medical Superintendent any complaint against any officer, nurse, employee, or patient, and not to subordinates in any department where the person is on duty.

16. Patients admitted to either general, private, or semi-private wards, shall be placed under the physician, surgeon or specialist who is on duty at the time, each patient being admitted in regular rotation. Patients shall not have the privilege or right to select their own medical or surgical attendant, except when by special and mutual consent, arrangements have been made regarding their attendance with a member of the Staff of their own choice, before becoming a patient in the Hospital.

17. Paying patients may in this way, only, select and employ any member of the Staff to attend them. All such terms and arrangements regarding such extra attendance must be made, and thoroughly understood by such patient, before being admitted to the Hospital under any special member of the Staff.

18. Members of the Visiting Medical Staff shall not claim compensation from patients treated or attended by them in the wards of the Hospital or from any out-door patient, except when in strict accordance with regulations in rules 16 and 17.

EXTERN STAFF FOR OUT-DOOR DEPARTMENT.

PHYSICIANS AND SURGEONS TO OUT-PATIENTS.

1. The Department for out-patients shall be under the care of the Physicians and Surgeons to out-patients.

2. The Physicians and Surgeons to out-patients shall, directly after their appointment, mutually arrange their respective days and orders of service with the Medical

Superintendent, which arrangements shall be subject to the approval of the Trustees.

3. The Physicians and Surgeons to out-patients shall be in attendance in their respective departments for the treatment of such out-patients as shall be unable to pay for medical or surgical treatment at their homes, in each week, as follows, viz. :—

MEDICAL AND SURGICAL.—Every day, except Sunday, between the hours of 1.30 and 2.30.

OPHTHALMIC.—Every day, except Sunday, at 2.30.

DISEASES OF THE SKIN.—Wednesday, between the hours of 1.30 and 2.30.

DISEASES OF THE EAR.—Every day, except Sunday, at 2.30.

SPECIAL DISEASES OF WOMEN.—Monday and Thursday, at 2.30, in Pavilion.

DISEASES OF THE THROAT AND NOSE.—Every day, except Sunday, at 2.30.

ELECTRICAL TREATMENT.—Monday, Wednesday and Friday, at 2.30.

4. Any Physician or Surgeon to out-patients, who shall be prevented from attending for a period exceeding one week in the term appointed for him, shall give notice to the Medical Superintendent, who shall arrange for one of the other Physicians or Surgeons to out-patients, as the case may be, to attend the service in his stead.

5. Any Physician or Surgeon to out-patients, finding himself unable to fulfil his regular daily appointment, shall immediately send notice of his inability so to do to the Medical Superintendent, who, if possible, shall procure the attendance of one of the other Physicians or Surgeons in his stead. Record shall be made of the Physician and Surgeon to out-patients making each regular visit, which record shall be open to the inspection of the Trustees.

7. No major operations shall be performed in the surgical departments for out-patients, except in cases of emergency. Whenever an out-patient requires such treatment or operation as may confine him for a time in the Hospital,

his case shall be referred to the Medical Superintendent for admission to Hospital.

8. All out-door patients recommended for admission as in-door patients, by any of the out-door Physicians, Surgeons or Specialists, shall, when admitted, be placed under the care of the Medical or Surgical officer in rotation then on duty.

9. Members of extern Staff are permitted to attend patients in private or semi-private wards, which they desire to send to the Hospital under their own care.

.MEDICAL AND SURGICAL ASSISTANTS.

The Trustees, with a view of increasing the facilities for more extensive clinical bed-side teaching, may appoint annually from the extern staff, certain members to act as medical or surgical assistants, subject to the following rules :—

1. Assistants may, during the temporary absence from the city or illness of the chief (with the consent only and on the full responsibility of the chief), visit such cases in the wards as may be desired by the chief, and may also, with the concurrence of the chief, give clinical instruction at the bed-side to limited numbers of students in small classes, not exceeding fifteen or twenty at any one clinic.

2. Assistants shall have due regard and consideration for the condition and disease of the patients, as to the length of time such patients shall be submitted to physical examinations, etc.

3. Assistants shall not perform surgical operations during the presence of their chiefs in the city, and shall not, except during the absence of the chief from the city, or when detained by illness, perform any major operation in the Hospital, and then only after a regular consultation of the Staff, and with the advice and consent of the majority of the Staff present.

TORONTO GENERAL HOSPITAL.

RULES FOR CLASSES AND OPERATIONS IN THEATRE.

MONDAYS	3.30	Clinical Lecture.
TUESDAYS	2.30	Surgical Operations.
WEDNESDAYS	1.30	Skin Clinic.
THURSDAYS	3.30	Clinical Lecture.
FRIDAYS	2.30	Surgical Operations.
SATURDAYS		Special Operations.

Attention of the Medical Staff is called to the following regulations regarding operations in Hospital :—

Regular operations in Theatre commence at 2.30 sharp, on Tuesdays and Fridays.

Abdominal sections and major operations in Pavilion Operating Room shall be performed between 10 and 12 o'clock a.m., whenever possible, and not on Tuesday or Friday afternoons, except in cases of emergency, or when delay might prove dangerous to patient.

No capital operation shall be performed (except where delay might be dangerous to patient) without giving notice thereof to all members of the Consulting and Surgical Staff of the Hospital, nor without the concurrence of the majority of those present. The nature and position of operations to be performed shall also be determined in the same manner.

Members of the Staff are required to notify the Medical Superintendent of their intention to perform any operations, at least twenty-four hours before operating, so that due notice shall be posted on Bulletin Board as soon as possible after notification.

Surgeons shall operate in the order of the notices given. No two operations shall be performed by any one surgeon *consecutively*, except when no other cases have been previously arranged for, on the same day.

Should any surgeon not be on hand punctually and prepared to operate at time specified, the next case in order on Notice Board shall be proceeded with, without delay.

Cases (of which no previous notice has been given), shall be taken in rotation, according to the order of seniority of the surgeons present.

PATHOLOGISTS.

1. The Hospital Laboratories and Museum shall be under the care and superintendence of, and under the immediate charge of the Pathologists.

2. It shall be the duty of the Pathologists, if requested, to attend surgical operations in the Hospital, and to conduct *post mortem* examinations in the autopsy room, the examinations to be made as nearly as possible at stated hours, to keep a record of every autopsy, which shall show the name of the deceased, the disease, and the result of the examination. They shall also be responsible for the good order and clean condition of the autopsy rooms.

3. They shall make pathological, microscopical and chemical analyses, when necessary, and shall keep an accurate record thereof.

4. They shall collect, examine, prepare and deposit in the Cabinet all such specimens occurring in or presented to the Hospital, as are thought worthy of preservation, each with appropriate label and reference to the catalogue.

5. They shall keep an analytical catalogue of all the preparations and other articles in the cabinet, and shall therein briefly note the most important facts as far as ascertained in relation to specimens, with further reference, if necessary, to the case books of the Hospital.

6. They shall see that every article belonging to the morgue and cabinet is kept in proper order, and that no specimen worthy of a place in the cabinet shall on any account be removed permanently therefrom; but any member of the Medical Staff, for the purpose of study or illustration, may take from the cabinet any specimen, or collection of specimens, by properly notifying the Pathologist, and in case of his absence, the Medical Superintendent of the Hospital.

7. All pathological specimens occurring in the Hospital shall be at the disposal of the Medical Staff, but no specimen worthy of a place in the cabinet shall on any account be permanently removed from the Hospital.

8. All preparations, and other articles received for deposit in the cabinet, shall be considered the property of the Hospital; but such of them as are presented, may be marked by the name of the donor, or that of the individual by whom they are prepared or collected.

9. The cabinet shall at all times be accessible to the Trustees, Physicians and Surgeons, and Medical Superintendent of the Hospital.

10. They shall make autopsies with the assistance of the House Officers, and shall cause reports of every such examination to be recorded by the House Staff, registrars, or clinical clerks.

11. They shall preserve and arrange all morbid specimens for the Pathological Museum.

12. They shall attend and make *post mortem* examinations on the bodies of patients dying in the Hospital whenever in the opinion of the Physician or Surgeon who attended such patient, and of the Medical Superintendent, it shall be desirable so to do.

REGISTRARS.

The Registrars shall arrange with the Medical Superintendent regarding the division and allotment of work to be performed by each in different departments or wards.

(1) The Registrars shall have the supervision of the making and preservation of all clinical reports, histories and records of Hospital patients. (2) They shall see that the Clinical Clerks or House Staff keep full records of the cases and treatment of all patients in both Medical, Surgical and other departments of the Hospital, and shall classify and keep the individual bed-side histories and records of every patient when discharged. (3) They shall prepare, classify and keep written up regularly, all Medical and Surgical Statistics regarding the cases under treatment, and make up as required for the annual Government report, and shall classify the diseases of all patients under treat-

6

ment, with number of operations, results, mortality, etc.
(4) They shall carefully supervise the work of clinical
clerks, and shall correct all clinical notes and records to
the end, that they may give an accurate and detailed
report annually to the Board of Trustees of the work of
the Hospital.

DIVISION OF REGISTRAR'S WORK.

Statistics — Government Register, Diseases, Operations, Births, Deaths, etc.	Clinical Ward— Work and Notes.
Cases to October 1st. October.... November.. December..	
January.... February... March.	
April ..... May....... June.......	
July ...... August .... September	

MEDICAL MEN AND MEDICAL STUDENTS.

1. Members of the regular Visiting Staff may, on regularly appointed days, perform operations in the amphitheatre, and members of both the Medical and Surgical
Visiting Staff may likewise give instruction there in their
respective departments. For the purposes of instruction
they shall, subject to such restrictions as the Trustees
may deem necessary, have the privilege of introducing
patients, provided that in every case the attending Surgeon
or Physician shall certify that the patient may undergo
such examination and treatment without detriment, and
that the patient consent thereto. Due notice of the nature

of such operations or instruction shall, so far as practicable, be posted on the Notice Board in Main Hall.

2. When the amphitheatre is opened for operations and instruction, Physicians having received a degree of Doctor of Medicine, and students of one year's standing of any duly incorporated College or School of Medicine or Surgery, may be admitted in such numbers and on such regulations as the Trustees may from time to time determine. Whenever the Operating Surgeon or the Physician shall deem a case improper for consideration in the presence of students of both sexes, he may reserve such case for the close of his operation or lecture, and require the withdrawal of all male or female students, as the case may be. No female patient shall be taken into the amphitheatre without the attendance of a nurse (female).

3. Physicians and Medical Students, accompanying a member of the Staff in his Hospital visits or examinations in the wards, shall be limited to a number not exceeding twenty-five, and shall conform to such regulations as may from time to time be made, and shall further observe all such requests as to order and propriety as the attending Physicians, or Surgeons, or the Medical Superintendent may make.

4. Students and Physicians coming to the Hospital for instruction shall be admitted only at the regular hours of operations, lectures, or visiting. Such persons shall, when required, show to the doorkeeper or attendant, Session cards of admission or of invitation, issued in accordance with the above rules, and all cards or invitations so issued may at any time be revoked or suspended by the Trustees. All such cards or invitations shall be forfeited if transferred to or used by persons other than those to whom they were issued. The Medical Superintendent may compel the withdrawal of any person who violates the rules of good order or refuses to conform to the requirements of the Physician or Surgeon in attendance.

5. Members of the Staff shall not deliver clinical lectures in the wards or take students to the wards after five o'clock in the day or on Sundays.

MEDICAL STUDENTS.

Students of Medicine shall be allowed to attend the practice of the Hospital at stated times only, on payment of $24 for a perpetual ticket, $8 for a six months' ticket, or $5 for summer session ticket. No student who has not taken out a Hospital ticket, shall, on any pretence whatever, be allowed to visit the Hospital or witness any operation, or attend Clinical lectures.

RULES AND REGULATIONS FOR THE GUIDANCE OF MEDICAL STUDENTS, CLINICAL CLERKS AND SURGICAL DRESSERS.

1. Students shall enter by the rear door under the theatre, and remain in the theatre or students' waiting-room until required by the Medical Officer of the day either the theatre or the wards. No students (except clinical clerks) will be allowed in any other part of the Hospital, except when in attendance on one of the Medical Officers.

2. The use of tobacco, in any form, in the theatre or any part of the Hospital, and spitting on the floors, strictly prohibited. Any student infringing this rule, or in any way cutting, disfiguring or injuring the walls or seats of the theatre, or any part of the Hospital property, will incur the penalty of expulsion.

3. First and second rows of seats in theatre are reserved for third and fourth year students.

4. The floor of the operating theatre is for the exclusive use of the Hospital Medical Staff.

5. Certificates of attendance must be obtained at the end of every session from the Medical Superintendent.

6. Students are requested to keep a correct record of their attendance in their Hospital note books.

7. Third and fourth year students only are admitted in rotation to bedside clinics, in limited numbers.

8. Students shall not stand about in the main stairway, corridors, or wards, unless they are acting as clinical clerks

or surgical dressers, or accompanied by one of the Hospital Staff.

9. Students whose turn it is to visit the wards for bedside clinics shall remain in the operating theatre or students' waiting-room until informed of the arrival of the Physician or Surgeon whom they are to accompany.

10. Students shall not enter or leave the theatre when an operation is going on. This rule is imperative.

11. Students shall stand in an orderly manner around the patient during the bedside clinics. They shall not at any time sit or stand on the beds. The continuance of bedside instruction at the Hospital depends chiefly on the condition that all students preserve perfect order and discipline when in the wards.

12. Clinical clerks and surgical dressers shall visit their patients between the hours of ten and twelve o'clock every day, and at any other hour named by the Medical Superintendent or Resident Assistant in charge of the ward, and students shall at all times be subject to the supervision of the Resident Staff. Students shall not enter into conversation with the nurses or patients, excepting those patients allotted to them. If they receive any directions for patients from visiting Physicians or Surgeons they shall communicate with the Resident Assistants in charge of ward, and not with the nurses.

13. Clinical clerks shall visit their patients every day, and shall first take a complete history of the cases up to the date of admission, with condition at same date, and shall keep thereafter correct daily records. These records shall be neatly transcribed in the Hospital case-books kept for that purpose.

14. Surgical dressers shall also take histories and keep records of their cases, and should be present at times when dressings are applied or changed, and shall apply or change such dressings, only when requested to do so by Resident Assistants. They can always get full information of hours for attending the surgical patients by inquiring of the Resident Assistant of the ward.

15. Clerks or dressers, in cases of unavoidable absence, shall give due notice thereof beforehand to the Medical Superintendent or Resident Assistant.

16. Students shall not be entitled to certificates as clinical clerks or surgical dressers unless they have carefully observed the above rules.

17. Any infraction of these regulations shall be reported to the Medical Superintendent and visiting Physician or Surgeon, and any student guilty of such violation shall be prevented thereafter from visiting the wards.

18. Students who do not receive the full benefit of the privileges they are entitled to under these regulations should report to the Medical Superintendent.

The following declaration of attendance must be signed by each student, before receiving Hospital Certificate:

No....... (DECLARATION OF ATTENDANCE.)

TORONTO GENERAL HOSPITAL.

I, the undersigned,.....................Student in Medicine, do hereby solemnly declare that I have attended the practice of the Toronto General Hospital at least ....times during the...........months, Session 189 , and that I am justly entitled to a Certificate for such attendance.

Witness :................

––––

BURNSIDE LYING-IN DEPARTMENT.

STUDENTS.

1. The student's fee for the maternity branch shall be $8, which fee entitles him to be present at six maternity cases.

2. Students having certificates of attendance at one course of lectures on Midwifery can obtain tickets of admission for practical Midwifery for $8, which includes attendance at six cases.

3. Only fourth year students are allowed to attend the practice of the Maternity Hospital. No student shall be allowed to visit the Hospital except when accompanied by one of the Maternity Staff, or the Medical Superintendent.

4. Before being admitted to the wards every student must make the following declaration :—

5. The Medical Superintendent shall regulate the order, etc., in which students shall attend cases.

FORM OF DECLARATION TO BE SIGNED BY STUDENT BEFORE ENTERING THE WARD.

I, the undersigned Student of Medicine, do hereby solemnly declare, that I will not visit or be present at cases of confinement in the Burnside Lying-in Hospital when engaged in pathological operations, when recently engaged in dissecting, or when dressing putrid sores, under penalty of expulsion.

RULES FOR PATIENTS.

Chronic cases, cases of senile debility, insane persons, or incurables not admitted.

All money or valuables belonging to patients must be left with the Secretary on admission. On no other condition will the Hospital be responsible for any loss, however it may happen.

Conditions only upon which all persons are admitted or treated either as in-door patients or as out-door patients :

Persons seeking admission into the Toronto General Hospital as patients, receive medical, surgical and all other treatment entirely free of charge ; whatever they pay or is paid for them, being solely on account of actual board and maintenance. Whilst the care and attendance bestowed on all patients is not the less, on account of its being gratuitous, it is distinctly understood that every patient receiving such treatment must agree to and become subject to all the rules of the Institution, and must implicitly obey and observe all regulations and by-laws, and carry out all orders regarding general or individual treatment. They must not in any way endanger their own chances of recovery, nor the recovery of their fellow patients; and must as far as possible, help to maintain the regulations and discipline of the Hospital. It is on these conditions only that persons are admitted as patients, and when admitted, must obey all rules and regulations, as by accepting such service or treatment, they personally assume all risks and responsibilities, as the Hospital being a charitable Institution, the Trustees are not liable, under any circumstances, for any accident, injury or casuality of any kind which may · happen to or befall any patient, employee, visitor or other persons, in the exigencies of such an institution, whether caused by the acts of any of the employees, Staff, or otherwise.

1. Patients must be in their proper places in the wards at meal times and during the visits of the physicians and surgeons, and always at eight o'clock at night; and no patient shall leave the Hospital grounds at *any time,* or be absent at the hour of morning visit without special leave from the Medical Superintendent.

2. Patients must be quiet and exemplary in their behaviour, and conform strictly to the rules and regulations of the Hospital, and carry out all orders and prescriptions of the various officers of the establishment. No indecent or immoral conduct will be tolerated. The use of tobacco in any form is strictly prohibited. Loud talking or unnecessary noise of any kind in wards or corridors is forbidden.

3. Patients are not allowed in any way to interfere with or remove their diet cards or charts from the wards. Patients must not take away bottles, labels, or appliances when leaving the Hospital.

4. After 8 p.m. perfect quiet must be observed in the wards.

5. Such patients as are able, in the opinion of the Medical Superintendent, physicians and surgeons, shall assist in nursing others, or in such services as the Medical or Lady Superintendent may require.

6. No patient shall enter any ward except his own, the basement storey, laundry, operating theatre, or any of the officers' or attendants' rooms, except by permission of an officer of the Hospital. No male patient shall enter the women's wards, or any female patient the men's wards.

7. Patients in private wards may be visited by their friends at any suitable hours in the day-time. Friends remain with patients over night only by special permission of Medical Superintendent, who may in all cases exercise discretionary powers as to excluding or admitting visitors.

8. No eatables or liquors of any kind shall be taken into wards by visitors; but if brought by them must be left with the head nurse, marked with the name of the patient for whom they are intended; to be examined by the medical officer, who will allow or refuse their use as he may think proper.

9. Any person bringing liquor into Hospital or grounds, or found intoxicated, will be discharged.

10. Private ward patients and female patients are allowed the use of front grounds west of carriage-road.

11. Eye and ear patients have the exclusive use of the grounds in rear of eye and ear infirmary.

12. Whenever patients misbehave or violate any of the rules of the Hospital the Medical Superintendent shall remove or discharge them.

13. At the regular visits of the physician every patient must be in his place. If able to sit up he must sit on the chair in front of his bed and keep it until the end of the visit. And no patient shall wear his hat, converse, or make any noise while the physicians are in the ward.

14. Patients are expressly prohibited from, 1st, lying in bed without being undressed, either by day or night; 2nd, from talking in the wards after 8 o'clock p.m.; 3rd, going other rooms or wards without permission, or beyond the limits assigned in the yards for exercise; 4th, occupying the steps at the entrance door and sitting on the staircases within the house; 5th, wilful or careless injury to any of the furniture or other property of the Hospital.

7

15. Patients allowed out on a pass and remaining beyond the time specified, will be regarded as discharged, and they must make a satisfactory explanation to the Medical Superintendent before they can return to their wards.

16. Convalescent patients, without exception, must render such help in the general work of their wards as their condition will warrant, in response to the demands of the nurses.

N.B.—All money or valuables belonging to patients must be left with the Secretary on admission. On no other condition will the Hospital be responsible for any loss, however it may happen.

Clothing and other effects of patients dying or leaving the Hospital, will not be kept longer than three months. Clothes and all other effects not claimed by patients or their legal representatives within three months, will be given to poor and needy patients of the Hospital, according to the discretion of or under the directions of the authorities.

RULES AND REGULATIONS FOR PATIENTS IN THE MATERNITY HOSPITAL.

(The Burnside Branch of the General Hospital.)

1. Public ward patients shall be admitted not more than two weeks before their expected accouchement.

2. All maternity patients shall be admitted by the medical superintendent subject to the regulations laid down from time to time by the board of trustees.

3. Public ward patients, when they are well enough, shall rise at 6.30 a.m. in summer and 7 a.m. in winter; they shall be expected to make their own beds and assist in keeping the wards in order, etc., under the supervision of the nurse in charge.

4. Private ward patients shall give a satisfactory guarantee to the Medical Superintendent for the payment of all Hospital charges.

5. When in the Hospital, public ward patients shall wear only such clothes as the Hospital provides.

6. On no pretence whatever shall the mother leave the Hospital without taking the infant with her.

VISITORS.

No visitors allowed to Lying-in Department except on a written order from the Medical Superintendent's office.

FORM OF ADMISSION OF COUNTY OR PAYING PATIENTS.

To the Medical Superintendent, Toronto General Hospital:

Admit . . . .

as a patient, to Toronto General Hospital, subject to the Rules and Regulations of the Institution, and the Municipality of . . . . will be responsible for payment on account of maintenance, at the rate of forty cents per day, while . . he remains in the Hospital.

Dated . . . .

. . . .

Reeve or Mayor.

N.B.—Chronic cases, cases of senile debility, insane persons, or incurables, not admitted.

If this order be limited in period, it is hereby agreed that all expenses for the patient's return fare are included in the guarantee, and that patient will be removed on expiration of such order.

Conditions upon which all patients are admitted :—

Every patient must agree to and be subject to all the rules of the Institution, and must implicitly obey and observe all regulations and by-laws, and carry out all orders regarding general or individual treatment. It is on these conditions only, that patients are admitted, and by accepting such free treatment, they assume all risks and responsibilities which may occur in the exigencies of such an Institution ; whatever they pay or is paid for them, being solely on account of board and maintenance, and not for professional treatment or services. The Hospital being a charitable institution, the Trustees are not liable, under any circumstances, for any accident, injury or casuality of any kind which may happen to or befall any patient, employee, visitor or other persons, caused by the acts of any of the employees, members of the Staff, or otherwise. No patient shall leave the Hospital grounds at *any time* without special leave from the Medical Superintendent. The use of tobacco in any form is strictly prohibited. Patients in private wards must 'furnish at their own expense all stimulants and medical luxuries required or ordered.

Private, semi-private and general ward patients are admitted to any of the departments in the Hospital at the following weekly rates, payable in advance, according to location and size of ward':

Private Wards...... ....$10 00 to $12 00
Semi-private Wards ....$ 6 00 to $ 8 00
General Hospital Wards $2 80

N.B.—*All money or valuables* belonging to patients must be left with the Secretary on admission. On no other condition will the Hospital be responsible for any loss, however it may happen.

FOR ADMISSION OF CITY PATIENT TO THE TORONTO GENERAL HOSPITAL.

CERTIFICATE OF CLERGYMAN OR WELL-KNOWN CITIZEN.

Toronto..............189..

THIS IS TO CERTIFY that........:.................has been a resident of Toronto for the last ...:............. and that neither he nor his family is in a position to pay for Hospital maintenance at the rate of forty cents per day.

Name,............................. ......
Address, ...

P. S. —This Certificate must be returned to the Medical Health Officer, St. Lawrence Hall, 157 King Street East, as the City order of admission must be obtained before patient is removed to Hospital, except in cases of emergency.

PHYSICIAN'S CERTIFICATE.

Toronto,................189..

I HEREBY CERTIFY THAT ....
...:.............Street, is suffering from...........
which requires active treatment such as the General Hospital affords.

Name,...........................
Address, ...

N.B.—Chronic cases, insane persons, cases of senile debility or incurables not admitted.

P.S.—This Certificate must be returned to the Medical Health Officer, St. Lawrence Hall, 157 King Street East, as the City order of admission must be obtained before patient is removed to Hospital, except in cases of emergency.

OUT-PATIENTS.

1. All poor persons will daily receive advice *gratis* at the Hospital.

2. The medicine prescribed for them by the visiting Medical Officer will also be supplied to them *gratis* from the Hospital, if patient is unable to pay for medicine at a drug store.

3. The visiting Medical Officer, or the Medical Superintendent, will also perform any ordinary operation, or render such other ordinary service to the applicant as may be necessary in the case.

4. They shall not loiter about the Hospital premises, they shall come directly to the place appointed for their reception, and as soon as they have been advised and treated, and received the medicine prescribed for them (if any such has been prescribed), they shall leave the Hospital premises.

5. They shall not be advised, treated, or given medicine, if they wilfully disobey or neglect any advice or direction which may be given to them.

6. They shall attend the Hospital in as cleanly a condition, in person and dress, as their complaint and circumstances will permit; and they shall conduct themselves while at the Hospital in a quiet and orderly manner.

7. They shall be removed from the Hospital, and they shall not be received again at the Hospital, or be advised, treated, or furnished with medicine, if they wilfully violate any of the rules or by-laws of the Hospital.

8. All out-patients must be in the waiting-rooms of the

Hospital at half-past one o'clock daily, except Sundays, and remain in the waiting-room until prescribed for. Extern patients must furnish their own bottles and gallipots, and see that they are kept clean.

Eye and ear cases admitted every day, except Sundays.... At 2.30 p.m.
Throat and nose cases admitted Mondays, Tuesdays,
    Thursdays and Fridays .... At 2.30 p.m.
Special diseases of women, Mondays and Thursdays ...... At 2.30 p.m.
Diseases of the skin, every Wednesday .... At 1.30 p.m.
Cases for electrical treatment, Mondays, Wednesdays and
    Fridays .... At 2.30 p.m.

The out-door free service is for the benefit of the poor only, and not for patients able to pay for medical advice and medicines.

9. Extern patients are subject to all rules, regulations and obligations of the Hospital, and by accepting free treatment assume all risks and responsibilities which may occur during their attendance at the Hospital.

RULES FOR VISITORS.

1. Visitors admitted on Tuesdays, Fridays and Saturdays from 2 to 5 p.m. *only*.

2. Clergymen or readers admitted daily between the hours of 3 and 5 p.m. This being a general Hospital, no patient can be constrained to hear any religious service or reading, unless he or she personally desire it, and is able safely to attend to it. All such readings and service shall be carried on so as not to interfere with those patients for whom the same is not intended, or who do not desire to listen. Visitors will kindly see the necessity of reading or talking on *religious* matters to patients of their own denomination *only*. The religion of each patient will be found on a card placed over every bed. Singing will be permitted in the Hospital theatre only, which can always be used when not required for other purposes.

3. For reasons that are obvious, visitors are requested to see the nurse before entering any ward.

4. Visitors are strictly prohibited from giving any article

of food, fruit, or luxuries to any patient. Any luxuries (intended for particular patients) can be left with the Lady Superintendent, who will be glad to distribute them under direction of the Medical Superintendent.

5. Visitors are requested not to interfere with the discipline of the Hospital by giving orders to nurses or patients.

6. Visitors are requested not to converse with patients concerning their medical or surgical treatment, and particularly regarding their individual diseases.

7. At the entrance of any of the medical men into a ward, visitors will retire if necessary.

8. Visitors are requested to leave the wards promptly at 5 o'clock, at the ringing of the bell.

9. Visitors desiring to make any complaints will kindly communicate with the Medical Superintendent.

10. Patients in private wards can be visited daily at reasonable hours, between 10 a.m. and 8 p.m. It is not desirable that more than two persons should visit a patient on the same day.

11. In cases of alarming illness the following card is sent immediately to the relatives or friends :—

TORONTO GENERAL HOSPITAL.

. . . . 189

. . . . Ward . . . . is considered *dangerously* ill. This card will admit you at reasonable times outside of the regular appointed visiting hours. Friends must keep themselves informed as to the condition of this patient without further notice.

☞ N.B.—Each visit must be limited in time, and friends must leave when requested by the nurse in charge. When this patient ceases to be dangerously ill, friends must come at regular visiting hours.

. . . . *Medical Superintendent.*

. . . .

12. The record of the religion on the card of every patient is intended for the convenience of clergymen of the same denomination only, and the officials of the Hospital are forbidden to allow any interference with or alteration of the records on these cards.

CERTIFICATE OF DEATH.

Undertakers or friends must obtain Certificate of Death from Medical Superintendent's Office. The Keeper will not deliver any body except on presentation of card properly signed.

As far as possible all bodies should be removed during business hours, and *no body can be taken from Morgue between 10 P.M. and 7 A.M.* The Keeper will return all cards to the Office on the first day of each month.

Remarks :

....

....

Date...

Deliver to ....

the body of...

....

———

Received the body of ....

....

Signature...

———

GENERAL RULES.

I.—No person shall attempt to regulate temperature in the wards by interfering with windows, registers or ventilators. Any patient so interfering will be immediately discharged from the Hospital. All such matters requiring attention should be reported to the office, and the Engineer will be sent promptly to render the necessary service.

II.—Pulling the elevator from one floor to another, however short the distance, is positively forbidden. The elevator must at all times be started from the floor where it has stopped by using the rope inside the car.

8

III.—Smoking and the use of tobacco will not be allowed in any portion of the Hospital buildings, except in the boiler room.

IV.—No instruments, apparatus or supplies, medical or surgical, shall be loaned or allowed to be taken outside the Hospital for private use, except by special permission of the Medical Superintendent, who alone may make exceptions to this rule in particular cases.

V.—Wines, liquors and other stimulants must be issued only on the order of the House Physician or House Surgeons, and noted in the diet book provided for that purpose.

VI.—Each order must specify the name of the patient for whom it is issued, and the amount required. No liquor shall be kept in bulk in any ward of the Hospital, except eight ounces of whiskey or brandy in the Emergency ward, and the same amount in the Operating Theatre, for cases of emergency, and there under lock, entrusted to the nurse on duty.

VII.—Resident officers and all employees of the Hospital shall perform such duties as the Medical Superintendent shall require at any time.

VIII.—It shall be the duty of all night attendants to guard during the night against any violation of the rules of the Hospital; and should such occur, or any circumstances requiring attention, they must report them immediately, or early in the morning, as the case may be, to the Medical or Lady Superintendent.

IX.—The officers and all employees are enjoined to be regular at their meals, as punctuality in this matter is considered essential to the discipline of the Hospital.

X.—All lights, except in the wards, entries, office, halls, boiler rooms, officers' and Physicians' rooms, are required to be extinguished at half-past ten o'clock p.m. at the latest. Reading in bed at night is not allowed, either to patients or to any person connected with the establishment in any capacity. A second breach of this rule will render the offender liable to immediate expulsion.

XI.—The telephone can be used by nurses and employees

on special occasions only, and then by permission of Medical or Lady Superintendent.

XII.—A careful record must be kept of patients' clothing, and diligence exercised to secure the return of all articles sent to the laundry or disinfecting tank. If such articles are not returned in due season, a prompt investigation must be made by those in charge.

XIII.—On the death of a patient all property (including clothing) must be delivered to the Head Nurse. Before a body is sent to the Morgue it should be carefully inspected and all jewelry and other valuables removed, either by the nurse in charge or by the ward-tenders.

SPECIAL RULES TO BE OBSERVED IN CASE OF FIRE.

1. Should a fire occur in any part of the Hospital buildings, blow the nearest fire alarm horn, telephone the Main Office, notify the Engineer, and use the nearest hose or water pails. Before turning on water, see that the hose is not twisted or kinked.

2. On an alarm of fire at any hour, all mechanics, gardeners, workmen and male employees (not on duty in the wards), shall report at once in Main Hall, and receive instructions from the officers of the Hospital on duty at the time.

3. All officers, nurses and employees are obliged to make themselves familiar with the use of the fire hose and all other fire appliances ; such instruction must be obtained from the Engineer as soon as possible after entering the Hospital service.

4. On an alarm of fire by day or by night, all house officers, nurses and employees, shall report at once in their respective wards or other places of duty, and be ready, if necessary, to assist in the removal of patients to places of safety.

5. All officers, nurses and employees of the Hospital are required, on retiring at night, to place their lanterns, clothes and boots close to their beds, so as to be able to dress quickly and render assistance as soon as possible after alarm of fire is given.

6. Life saving Nets, Ropes, Axes, Lanterns, Pails, Crow Bars, Sledge Hammers, Hose Keys, Wrenches, Saws, Ladders and Chemical Fire Extinguishers are kept in the Main Hall ready for instant use.

7. A special fire alarm box, No. 252, directly connected with all city fire halls east of Yonge street, is situated in Main Hall. This alarm is to be rung for fire in Hospital premises only.

8. The first care is to preserve the lives of the patients, and those in charge of them, must do what is best under the circumstances to accomplish this, in the safest manner possible. To prevent undue excitement, good order, coolness, and deliberation are necessary at all such critical times.

DIETARY FOR PATIENTS. *(Subject to changes at any time.)*

MILK DIET. Daily.—Milk, three pints; Bread, toasted if desired; Butter, Rice, Oatmeal, Corn Starch, or Farina.

FULL OR HOUSE DIET.

SUNDAY.	MONDAY.	TUESDAY.	WEDNESDAY.	THURSDAY.	FRIDAY.	SATURDAY.
BREAKFAST. Tea with Milk and Sugar. Bread and Butter.	**BREAKFAST.** Tea, with Milk and Sugar. Bread and Butter. Porridge and Milk.	**BREAKFAST.** Tea, with Milk and Sugar. Porridge of Oatmeal.	**BREAKFAST.** Tea, with Milk and Sugar. Bread, Toast, Butter. Porridge.	**BREAKFAST.** Tea, with Milk and Sugar. Bread and Butter. Porridge of Oatmeal.	**BREAKFAST.** Tea, with Milk and Sugar. Bread and Butter. Porridge of Oatmeal.	**BREAKFAST.** Tea, with Milk and Sugar. Bread and Butter.
DINNER. Roast Beef, or Mutton, Potatoes, Bread, Pudding.	**DINNER.** Soup, or Stewed Meat, Vegetables, Bread, Pudding of Bread, Rice, or Tapioca.	**DINNER.** Beef, Roast or Boiled. Potatoes. Bread, and Rice Pudding.	**DINNER.** Roast Beef, or Mutton, Boiled. Potatoes. Bread. Pudding.	**DINNER.** Boiled Corned Beef. Soup, or Vegetables. Bread. Pudding of Bread or Rice.	**DINNER.** Roast Beef or Mutton. Fish, Fresh or Salt. Potatoes, Beets or other Vegetables. Bread. Pudding.	**DINNER.** Roast Beef. Potatoes. Bread. Pudding of Bread or Rice.
SUPPER. Tea, with Milk and Sugar. Bread and Butter.	**SUPPER.** Tea, with Milk and Sugar. Bread and Butter.	**SUPPER.** Tea, with Milk and Sugar. Bread and Butter.	**SUPPER.** Tea, with Milk and Sugar. Bread and Butter.	**SUPPER.** Tea, with Milk and Sugar. Bread and Butter.	**SUPPER.** Tea, with Milk and Sugar. Bread and Butter.	**SUPPER.** Tea, with Milk and Sugar. Bread and Butter.

EXTRAS.—In addition to the above, the following extras may be ordered by the visiting physicians and surgeons :—Milk, Beef Tea, Chicken Broth, Mutton Broth, Gruel, Oatmeal Mush, Corn Starch, Boiled Rice, Eggs, Beefsteak, Mutton-chop, and Chicken.

A small allowance of Milk and Beef Tea will be provided for each ward daily. The House Staff may order these articles by a signed special order in each case, when needed, for patients who enter in the intervals between the regular visits of the visiting physician or surgeon to whom the case is assigned.

All Wines and Liquors, Ale, Beer, etc., will be ordered by the visiting physicians and surgeons only, excepting in emergencies, when special orders for the same may be given by the house physician or surgeon, to be afterwards approved by the visiting physician or surgeon, as the case may be, or by the Medical Superintendent.

BURNSIDE LYING-IN HOSPITAL.

AMALGAMATED WITH TORONTO GENERAL HOSPITAL, 1877.—OPENED FOR RECEPTION OF PATIENTS, OCTOBER 1ST, 1878.

NUMBER OF BIRTHS IN THE BURNSIDE LYING-IN HOSPITAL

From October 1st, 1878, to September 30th, 1879....	159
" " 1879, " " 1880....	159
" " 1880, " " 1881....	142
" " 1881, " " 1882....	122
" " 1882; " " 1883....	148
" " 1883, " " 1884....	158
" " 1884, " " 1885....	162
" " 1885, " " 1886....	182
" " 1886, " " 1887....	162
" " 1887, " " 1888....	183
" " 1888, " " 1889....	192
" " 1889, " " 1890....	171
" " 1890, " " 1891....	156
" " 1891, " " 1892....	119
" " 1892, " " 1893....	121
" " 1893, " " 1894....	128
" " 1894, " " 1895....	158

Total...........................2622

It is a white brick structure with two storeys and basement. In latter, are the servants' apartments, kitchen and pantries, patients' dining and sitting-rooms. On the first floor are rooms for students, medical assistants, nurses' apartments, and private wards. On the second floor, are the public wards and other rooms.

THE PAVILION.

The "Pavilion," for special diseases of women, erected
in 1882. Is. built of white brick, with two storeys, and
is situated in the northern portion of the grounds behind
the western division of the Hospital. An extensive addition has lately been made, so that at present it has a capacity of forty beds. It is devoted to special diseases of
women and abdominal surgery, is completely isolated,
heated by the Smead & Dowd system, and equipped with
all modern conveniences in lighting and ventilating, with
examining and operating rooms, public and private wards,
kitchens, pantries, bathrooms, portable baths, etc., and a
dispensary for extern patients, for special diseases of
women only.

BENEFACTORS.

Bequests and Donations to Hospital Trust of sums of $400 and upwards.

Copy of names inscribed on Tablet in main entrance hall :

1861	Alexander Sanderson	$ 400
1867	George Michie	2,000
1869	John G. Walker	400
1871	George Henry	2,000
1875	James Ferrier Gentle	5,000
1875	Erland Erlandson	15,000
1878	William Gooderham, Sr	4,500
1878	James G. Worts	4,500
1878	William Cawthra	4,500
1882	William Gooderham, Jr	2,000
1882	John Macdonald	500
1883	John Macdonald	500
1884	Executors of James Michie	5,000
1886	Executors of Margaret J. Roaf	1,000
1886	The R. B. Butland Bequest (estimated)	14,000
1887	Executors of Alexander McGregor	500
1889	Executors of John B. Lloyd	600
1890	Executors of James E. Drinkwater	1,500
1891	Executors of George Davison	1,500
1891	Executors of Hon. John Macdonald	2,000
1891	Executors of Rev. Father T. C. McMahon	2,820
1884 to 1891	Grand Trunk Railway Company	1,000
1892	Executors of late A. F. Fulton	5,000
1892	Executors of late Henry Buck	1,000

FORM OF LEGACY.

TO THE TORONTO GENERAL HOSPITAL.

I give and bequeath to THE TORONTO GENERAL HOS-PITAL the sum of

.... Dollars

to be paid out of my personal estate, and if necessary in preference to all debts and bequests other than charitable bequests; and to be applied towards the purposes for which said Hospital was incorporated, and the signature of the Chairman and Secretary for the time being shall be sufficient discharge therefor.

(To be witnessed by two persons.)

www.ingramcontent.com/pod-product-compliance
Lightning Source LLC
Chambersburg PA
CBHW021536270326
41930CB00008B/1283